Insight Text Guide

by

Pamela Williams

(BAHons)

Katherine Thomson's

Diving for Pearls

This edition first published in 1999 by
Insight Publications Pty Ltd
ACN 005 102 983
PO Box 130
Drouin Victoria 3818
Australia.
☎ 03 5625 1701

Editing by Iris Breuer

Design and DTP by Geoffrey Heard & Associates ✆ (03) 9583 0788

Printed by Shannon Books, Bayswater, Victoria.

Williams, Pamela

Insight text guide: Katherine Thomson's Diving for Pearls

ISBN 1 875882 32 4

1. Thomson, Katherine, 1955- Diving for Pearls. 2. Thomson, Katherine, 1955- . Criticism and interpretation. I. Title. (Series: Insight text guide).

The editors and publishers wish to acknowledge the kind permission of Currency Press, Australia, to reprint extracts from *Diving for Pearls* by Katherine Thomson.

CONTENTS

INTRODUCTION

***In 1990, Katherine Thomson described her play,* Diving for Pearls[1]*, as 'a middle-aged love story against a background of industrial relations and privatisation'*[2].**

According to the program for the Sydney Ensemble Theatre's 1998 production, Katherine Thomson's play 'forces us to question the values of wealth, power and production as the motivating force in our lives'.[3] Critics have described it as 'a story of dreams and disappointments, government folly and failed businesses'[4], and 'an attempt to dramatise the things working people suffer as a result of retrenchment, lack of opportunity, too little money'[5]. So, what is the primary concern of *Diving for Pearls*? Simply put, Thomson's play is a social drama that looks closely at the 'human cost' of living in Australia in the 1990s when governments and businesses were intent on industrial reform through a policy of economic rationalism. Frequently industrial reformers overlook the rather unsavoury fact that those initiatives that will best serve the 'profit margin' of the accountants' balance sheets are all too often the ones most likely to cause widespread economic and human devastation.

Thomson's motivation for writing her play came about while she was undertaking some research for an ABC documentary about the New South Wales coastal industrial city of Wollongong. She became 'so emotionally involved that [she] decided to turn it into a play'.[6] By weaving together a strong political message and the doomed love affair of Den and Barbara, Thomson places a very human face on some of the most vulnerable members of Australian society who are usually only 'visible' as statistics. Her naturalistic approach compels us to question our ideas about free trade, Australian egalitarianism, loyalty, family relationships, security, and even the value of the simple human tendency to 'dream'.

---

1 Katherine Thomson, *Diving for Pearls*, Currency Press, Paddington, NSW, 1992. All references to the text are to this edition.

2 Interview with Katherine Thomson by Jo Litson in *The Australian*, 31 May 1990, p. 9.

3 Quoted by David Allen in 'Doomed love has universal appeal', *The Australian*, 5 June 1998, p. 15.

4 Candida Baker, ' 'Pearls' from Geelong', *The Age*, 26 March, 1991, p. 14.

5 Peter Craven, 'Cardboard cut-outs cast adrift in the shallows', *The Australian*, 4 April 1991, p. 9.

6 Interview with Katherine Thomson by Jo Litson in *The Australian*, 31 May 1990, p. 9.

CONTEXT & BACKGROUND

Restructuring and Redundancy

If, in order to stay in business, an organisation must streamline its procedures, sharpen its practices, and run in a lean and efficient manner, changes must be made.

During the period in which *Diving for Pearls* is set, Australian industry was facing one of its biggest challenges. Computer technology was fast revolutionising the way in which things were made, and production lines were becoming increasingly mechanised and specialised, reducing labour costs and boosting manufacturing capacities. Competition for international markets was high, so in order to achieve that vital 'competitive edge', companies restructured or closed down. Many companies employed teams of experts to carry out feasibility studies and to assist management in deciding whether to restructure their operations or simply to close them down. Accordingly, we see Ron's firm of consultants called in to assist the government in deciding the future of the State Engineering Works. However, all too often, as Thomson shows us, the consultants' purpose is merely to provide the supporting evidence that will justify the course of action the client has already decided to take (p. 70).

In cases where legitimate restructuring is to take place, consultants are asked to 'target' those employees most suitable for retraining (p. 34) and those others who are unsuitable for reasons of age, poor physical condition, or lack of ability who should, consequently, be dismissed (p. 48).

It is fair to assume that Den was offered a redundancy payment because he was a talented labourer (p. 17) who would undoubtedly have become a valuable employee had there been any intention of keeping the Works operating. Also called 'golden handshakes', these payments are made to people whose employment is terminated through no fault of their own, and is due solely to the large-scale changes taking place within an organisation. Legitimate payments are usually large enough to compensate for the loss of earnings a person will incur whilst seeking a new position.

However, in Den's case, the sum he is offered is merely a token gesture (p. 73) to facilitate the smooth sale of the Works.

Economic Rationalism

A key concept in enabling Australia to be competitive in trading internationally, 'economic rationalism' (or microeconomic reform as it is more formally known), is the pursuit of making more product for less cost.

Currently, in the late 1990s, we have seen this practice cross over from the manufacturing industry into commerce, education, and other service industries, with the result that less people are doing the same or even more work, in order to maintain the level of service that their clientele (and management) demand. The consequences entailed in this way of operating in terms of workplace conditions and employment opportunities for individuals are usually pretty grim. They include reduced numbers of 'permanent' and full-time jobs, more people forced into the casual and part-time labour pool, fewer jobs for those less highly skilled members of the work force, reduced job prospects for the young and 'middle-aged', serious erosion of workplace conditions and job satisfaction. Jacko's suicide can be seen as the direst result of being pushed out of the permanent work force, and Barbara's description of her job in the garment manufacturing trade is a good example of how bad conditions can get:

> BARBARA: I got a job all right. In at Diamond's this time, sewing up little baby's dingo suits. First bell at 8.14, last bell at 4.14. No going to the toilet an hour after morning tea or an hour after lunch (p. 13).

Privatisation

Another useful tool in the pursuit of microeconomic reform is privatisation. This strategy has become increasingly popular during the '90s and Australians have witnessed the 'selling off', either partially or completely, of government-owned buildings and corporations such as Telstra, the supply organisations for gas, water and electricity, and even the Commonwealth Unemployment Service. By shifting the responsibility for the successful running of these vital services and facilities to private enterprise, the government undoubtedly makes substantial savings. However, because the private sector must operate at a profit, the brunt of the financial burden has to be shouldered by all Australians, regardless of their ability to pay and whether they still have a job. Often, as Davis and Dixon decide to do with the State Engineering Works, they simply strip the enterprise of useful or saleable items and then sell the real estate (p. 70).

Diving for Pearls ***encourages us to recognise that although privatisation may enable the government to realise large sums of money for the assets they sell off 'up front', it is arguably a 'quick fix'.***

Not only does the government lose valuable sources of on-going revenue, it is also obliged to find the money for social security benefits for those who, as a consequence, will become members of the long-term unemployed, as well as cover the expense of subsidies so that these low-income earners can meet the costs of their rent, and gas, electricity and water bills.

GENRE, STYLE & STRUCTURE

Genre

An active imagination is the key to successfully reading drama. Because it is a genre that is specifically written for performance, it is important to visualise the surroundings, people, and action as you read. Take careful note of the stage directions, character notes and playwright's instructions on how to stage the play, in order to keep the play alive in your 'mind's eye'.

Diving for Pearls as Social Drama

Diving for Pearls deals with issues that relate to our contemporary society and our everyday lives, and Thomson's realistic portrayal of the world that Den and Barbara inhabit tends to dispel the myth that Australian society is not a 'class' conscious one. Although in essence a tragedy, Thomson uses irony and comic interludes throughout the play in order to avoid losing her audience in a sea of misery and despair. Some of these border on slapstick — Barbara and Marj at the Leagues Club (pp. 27-32); Verge and the 'savouries' (p. 62) — while others utilise a clever and subtle playing around with words and their meanings — 'exceptional extras/optional extras' (p. 23); 'principle/principal' (p. 79).

Style

Thomson notes that 'almost all her plays are set in a gritty, realistic work environment'[7] and her use of the naturalistic style helps audiences to feel that what they are seeing — 'witnessing' — is real. In extreme forms, naturalism demands that the set, as well as the costumes, dialogue, and behaviour of the characters matches what we are accustomed to in our everyday world.

Although not specifically stated, the play is obviously set in Wollongong, with the dialogue aptly portraying the ordinary, everyday Australian use of language, realistically littered with appropriate colloquialisms and swearing.

Thomson does not slavishly follow the naturalistic conventions, however, as we can see from the staging instructions (refer Author's Note prefacing Act 1) where she describes a rather abstract acting space. Den's monologues in which the theatre audience assumes the 'role' of the audience at the public speaking class is another non-naturalistic technique.

Symbols

It is also important to note the use of symbols in the play. There is the fairly obvious symbolism such as the uses of **pink** (Barbara's 'rose-coloured' glasses) which make the International Resort Hotel the focus of Barbara's dreams and represent her aspirations for a better life, and **the noose** that Ron discovers in the Works. There is also the recurring presence, both seen and heard, of **the tuba** which represents Den's father's voice, the voice of the simple, straightforward working man with few illusions who spoke his mind and never trusted those in authority. The tuba appears at those moments in the play where the characters are in danger of losing, or have already lost, the important grounding connection with their working past. **The hill** on which the action begins and ends is also symbolic. Not only does it represent how the environment has been sacrificed in the pursuit of wealth, it also reminds us that coastal industrial cities are, in themselves, contradictions because they consist of not only factories, chimneys, and slag-heaps but also wide, sandy beaches and beautiful rainforests.

Structure

Diving for Pearls ***is a two-act play, with each act containing fifteen scenes. The scenes are 'filmic' in nature, being mostly short and tending to dissolve into one another.***

In the first act we get to know the characters, their dreams and aspirations, watching the development of their relationships and their discovery of new hope for the future. Although Act 1 ends on a note of supreme optimism, we are not totally unprepared for the atmosphere of destruction, disappointment and disillusionment that pervades Act 2. In keeping with the conventions of modern drama, the play's ending is not one of unequivocal resolution. Although the characters are, realistically, worse off than when we first met them, the ending is not entirely pessimistic: Barbara's tenacious optimism is evident again, Den is looking ahead to the time when 'everything's settled' (p. 87) and we know that Marj has reconsidered both her opinion of Den and her ideas of what is 'right' for Verge. As one reviewer wrote: '*Diving for Pearls* is partly a memorial to the Jackos who did not survive...but it is also a tribute to the Barbaras and Dens who battled on'.[7]

7 Review by Elizabeth Perkins, *Australasian Drama Studies*, No. 24, April 1994, pp. 197-200.

SCENE-BY-SCENE ANALYSIS 

Note that each act is divided into short sections or episodes. For ease of reference these are set out here as numbered scenes.

Act One

Scene 1 (pp. 1-7)

Barbara and Den discuss Jacko's death, the city in which they live, and their respective lives. Important background material supplied.

This scene is set on a hilltop overlooking the town and the church where Barbara and Den have just attended Jacko's funeral. Through their conversation, Den and Barbara not only give some idea of the sort of people they are, but they also inform the audience about the economic and social climate of the coastal industrial city in which they both live and work.

During their exchange, we discover that once vital industries have either closed down or undergone a process of down-sizing which has impacted in various ways on the city's inhabitants. For Barbara, the relocation of the abattoirs caused her husband Barry to join the ranks of the long-term unemployed, a factor which played a significant role in the break-up of her marriage. For Jacko, the reduction in staffing levels at the steelworks ultimately led to his suicide.

However, the shift in the city's economy has not been negative for everyone. The once-pitied 'mob from the Northern Beaches' (p. 3), 'living in their poky little shacks' (p. 3) have suddenly found that they own prime real estate, and with cottages selling for a 'quarter of a million dollars' (p. 3) they are enjoying a very different life-style through their new-found wealth.

First Impressions of Barbara

Barbara appears to be dissatisfied not only with her life, but also with the place in which she lives it. She emerges as someone who is very familiar with disillusionment, which may explain the 'tough cookie' attitude she adopts. In this scene, she is obviously upset and angry, due largely to the church service she has just attended. Her sarcastic comments to herself as the scene opens reveal her cynical attitude towards the local 'establishment' and its rituals. She sees hypocrisy in the fact that the priest referred to Jacko as 'John' ('Don't bother getting a person's name right — bloody priests' [p. 1]), and the omission of any reference to Jacko's death being suicide she interprets as a deliberate attempt to hide the facts: 'They want to find a way to cover it all up' (p. 4).

However, the resentment the audience senses in Barbara seems to be too strong to be attributed merely to the upset and sadness of Jacko's funeral, and is more likely to be the result of disappointment due to her lack of money and social standing. She is obviously envious of those whose homes are now in the sought-after suburbs, and her observation that, 'You could divide this city in half' (p. 3) demonstrates that she sees these people as the 'haves', and herself as one of the 'have-nots'.

First Impressions of Den

Throughout the scene, Den tries to wrest control of the conversation from Barbara and shift it onto a more personal level. This alerts the audience to the unfinished business between the two of them and to the fact that Den would like to pursue a relationship with Barbara, however, Barbara's resistance is obvious.

What we learn in this scene about Den and his approach to life comes to us in terms of Barbara's descriptions and memories of Jacko. Barbara's opinion of Den seems to be that he is not of Jacko's calibre: Barbara states that Jacko was Den's 'opposite' (p. 3). Den does appear to be tentative and unsure of himself and, as he says himself, he and Jacko were not 'mates' (p. 2) at work, but he does come across as thoughtful and kind. Where Jacko played cards at lunchtime, Den preferred 'a quiet corner' and the company of a 'cowboy novel' (p. 3). While Jacko went about being a trouble-maker and 'shaking things up' (p. 3), Den's preference (according to Barbara) was to 'steer clear' (p. 3) because he preferred to keep his head down and avoid trouble.

What this reveals is that Den is inclined to think a bit before taking action, rather than jumping in feet first like Jacko. Something which Den reveals to the audience (and which Barbara appears to miss) is that, in fact, Jacko's campaign to expose nationally the plight of the steelworkers was unnecessary and pretty futile: 'They were always going to keep fifty per cent of us' (Den: p. 4).

Scene 2 (pp. 7-11)

Den's brother-in-law, Ron, arrives at the State Engineering Works. He alerts Den to the fact that major improvements are planned for the Works.

In this scene Thomson again uses the strategy of comparison to expose more of Den's personality. The dialogue between Ron and Den highlights the differences between them, and the audience is exposed to, and asked to think about, notions of ambition, achievement, and success.

Ron and Den

Clearly, Ron and Den are not merely relatives. Rather, they are old friends who have a shared past which is demonstrated by their ability to pick up their familiar 'Denny/Ronny' joke (p. 7). We discover that Ron and Den both started at the 'Works' twenty-five years ago as temporary employees. Unlike Den who has never moved on, Ron has pursued an education and a professional career although, ironically, his achievements appear to have brought him in a full circle back to the Works where he started. Emblematic of Ron's circular journey is the trolley he pushes with the '*recalcitrant wheel...which at times leads him around in circles*' (p. 7).

In contrast to Den, who is at pains to emphasise how uninformed and unimportant he is, Ron's confidence in his abilities appears to be high. He takes great delight in relating to Den how he got the better of the government Minister and we can see that, like Barbara, he has little respect for those in authority. His pride in the fact that he is 'still a hoon' (p. 10) is obvious.

However, Ron is the only one in his firm without a Harvard MBA and his sense of inferiority comes through when he makes a slip of the tongue in relation to his enjoyment of his job: 'Happy as a fish out of wa — pig in shit, whatever it is' (p. 10). Further, unlike Jeannie (his wife and Den's sister), who is 'right at home in Perth' with the 'cowboys and wankers' (p. 9), Ron is not.

Ron's optimism is in direct contrast to Den's pessimism: 'Now, you were never a live wire mate but you used to have a bit more spark' (p. 10). The general air of disintegration is picked up from the previous scene: the trains are 'packed away mostly' (p. 10), the wild birds have disappeared along with the 'bit of bush up the back' (p. 11) and the birds 'in the aviary died. About a week before the old man' (p. 11).

Scene 3 (pp. 11-13)

Den visits Barbara at her boarding house and gives her the happy coat he received from Ron.

In this scene, Den makes some progress in breaking down the barriers Barbara has put up in her mind about his unsuitability as a partner for her. Den's timing is rather good as Barbara has just been obliged to take yet another boring job in a factory behind a sewing machine and is feeling that maybe she will never escape to a 'brand new life' (p. 12).

Barbara's room, which contains everything she owns, is cramped and messy and accordingly, she is disconcerted by Den's unexpected visit. Realising this, Den continues to press his advantage, observing that at his place he 'rattles about' (p. 11), making it plain to her that he has the potential to improve her life. By showing her the newspaper announcement about the planned changes to the Works and the promise of ongoing job security, he is again trying to tempt her to see him differently.

Barbara does admit that she has revised her opinion of Den, conceding that he has 'something nice' (p. 13) about him, but although his gift has taken her by surprise, she still clings to her opinion that he is 'too quiet' (p. 13). Viewing life as a 'race', she observes that he would 'never keep up' with her (p. 13).

Scene 4 (pp. 13-17)

Ron makes it clear to Den that he is determined to include him in the restructuring process — whether Den likes it or not.

Ron reveals that Den has both talent and skill but Den's lack of self-esteem is plain, and his reluctance to become involved in or to engage with the process of reorganisation demonstrates his lack of confidence in his own abilities. Avoidance appears to be Den's safety zone and he refuses to participate in the conversation Ron wants to have by holding forth on the mysteries of devon sandwiches. Although this discourse does not capture Ron's imagination, the audience can see that through having Den maintain the family tradition of the devon sandwich for lunch, Thomson is establishing how much he relies on the safety and security provided by the old, traditional ways.

Den is not comfortable with Ron's tendency to run management down, he is sceptical that any good can come out of the sort of action Ron is proposing, and he would rather be left well out of it. Ron, however, is determined that Den will participate in the restructuring process. Whether Ron has Den's interests at heart or his own, is not clear at this stage. Is he intent on assisting Den to improve his situation as a way of repaying him for his help in Ron's 'escape' from the Works, or is he motivated by a more self-interested desire to free himself, after all these years, from a sense of obligation?

Scene 5 (pp. 17-19)

Den and Barbara consummate their relationship and decide to become 'a couple'.

It is at this point in the play that Den's self-esteem starts to improve. His success in becoming Barbara's lover has boosted his confidence and his observation that people should 'stop being scared of each other' (p. 18) indicates his awareness that his reluctance to trust others has been holding him back.

Den hints that the reason he has stayed away from the public speaking classes is due to the presence of 'mostly estate agents and bank clerks' (p. 19). Barbara's advice that 'you don't take any notice of them' (p. 19) comes across as being the sort of common-sense approach that the overly diffident Den needs.

Barbara is still cautious and indicates that she has reservations about the ability of one person to totally fulfil another, but she seems to see more advantages in the situation than disadvantages: 'Oh, why not for heaven's sake. Why not?' (p. 18). Noting that fighting 'romance' causes it to 'blow up in your face' (p. 18), she points out that regardless, she will be maintaining her 'goals' (p. 18). While an audience might readily agree with the essence of her remarks, they would be a little uneasy about seeing the relationship between Barbara and Den as 'romantic', especially in light of Barbara's injunction that they should take things 'one step at a time' (p. 18).

Scene 6 (pp. 19-20)

Den returns to the public speaking class and gives a talk on trains and his grandfather.

Den's talk about trains can be interpreted as a metaphor of his life. The trains that he is most familiar with are the ones he helps to build at the Works and it is this kind of train that initially springs into his mind. These trains are meant for practical purposes — 'you wouldn't take a ride in what we build…they're not so interesting' (p. 20). When he moves on to discuss train journeys, he makes the observation that he has not 'done any' despite the fact that his grandfather left him some money for one (p. 20).

The image he gives of his grandfather's habit, when travelling, of always knowing 'at any given moment, precisely what direction the train was going in' (p. 20), indicates how much importance Den places on keeping a constant eye on where you are heading in life and the necessity of conforming — staying on the tracks. In terms of all of this Den, up to this point in the play, can be seen as having remained at the station all his life.

Scene 7 (pp. 21-25)

Barbara lays out her plans to Den for her new career and asks him to pay for her course at the Academy.

In this scene the train/journey motif is carried on. In Ron's appearance *within* the action but not *of* it, there is a discernible link to Den's talk in the previous scene. According to Ron, the Works will be making passenger trains instead of goods trains for transporting coal, and the opportunities to for staff to re-train and acquire new skills will be available for those who move quickly. His advice that Den should 'pick up a career path and move along the ladder. Your welder's ticket, electronics...' (p. 21) again raises an image of getting your journey 'on track', passing through the correct stations, and maintaining your direction.

Barbara is on the move. When Den reaches out to kiss her, her response is to throw him a pair of runners: where he seeks security and emotional bonds, she strives towards self-transformation and material success. The audience is reminded of Barbara's observation in scene 4 (p. 13) that life is a race.

This scene exposes the fundamental differences between Den's and Barbara's perceptions of how life should be lived.

Barbara is very motivated about improving the status and quality of her life. When she tells Den, 'I only want to go as far as the point' (p. 21), and he replies that the point 'is only as far as you can go' (p. 21), clearly Barbara sees her limitations only in terms of the goals she has set for herself, whereas Den sees his limitations as being fixed by outside forces that are beyond his control.

Den is rather dismayed at the cost of the course that Barbara wants to do at the Academy. In her 'sales pitch' to win Den over to the idea, Barbara talks of 'exceptional extras' (p. 23), conveying her view of them as an intrinsic part of the course; Den corrects her, designating them as 'optional extras' (p. 23), repositioning them as something you *choose* to do. Where Den describes the course as 'expensive' (p. 23), seeing it in terms of dollar outlay, Barbara views it as 'intensive' (p. 23), seeing it purely from the perspective of its benefit to her in the pursuit of her 'goals'.

At the close of the scene, Den has not reached a decision, but he does 'hang on' (p. 24) to the brochures Barbara has given him.

Scene 8 (p. 25)

Barbara's sister, Marj, appears for the first time, introducing the mystery of 'Virginia'. In this short scene two troubled and troubling relationships begin to emerge — namely, the difficult one between the sisters, Barbara and Marj, and the rather one-sided mother/daughter relationship between Barbara and Verge.

Clearly, Marj is a rather conservative and controlling person, who seems able to intimidate and dishearten Barbara merely by her presence. It is reasonable to suggest that they are not close.

Less explicit at this point is Virginia's place in the sisters' lives. The mother/daughter relationship remains ambiguous, mostly because, in the opening scene, Barbara has given the impression that she is childless with her comment: 'Not as if I was leaving any kids' (p. 6). Note that Thomson has already brought Virginia onto the stage between scenes 3 and 4 (*A girl walks along with her suitcase*...p. 13), but the audience was not informed, at the time, who she was, or how she fitted into the action.

Scene 9 (pp. 25-27)

Den and Ron resurrect the model train set and discuss Den's training for his new role at the Works.

Despite the fact that Ron is constantly buoying up Den's confidence about his value in the workplace, Ron's enjoyment of the power inherent in his role at the Works, and over Den, is evident. Whether Den senses this or not, his query, 'You don't reckon you're not still a bit of a two bob lair' (p. 26) prompts such a boastful response from Ron that the audience is left in little doubt that he is, indeed, a 'lair'.

When Ron stands up and destroys one of the model railway's small cottages, this event foreshadows two important threats to Den's security. The first is the potential of Ron's approach to job restructuring to cause grave damage to Den at work; the second is Jeannie's intention to sell the house Den lives in, which has been his home for as long as he can remember.

The scene ends on an ironic note. When the 'new-look' Barbara appears, declaring that Den cannot expect to see her 'every day' (p. 27) because of her workload at the Academy, it is clear that Den is the one who has been taken advantage of. He is far from advantageously attaching himself to 'a wealthy woman' (p. 27) as Ron suggests. There is also a distinct change in Barbara's attitude towards Den now that he has paid for what she wanted.

Scene 10 (pp. 27-32)

It is Barbara's birthday and Marj and Barbara meet for lunch at the Leagues Club. They become so engrossed in fighting with each other that they never actually sit down and eat.

The audience realises that the lunch date is doomed when the two sisters arrive wearing identical dresses. That Barbara's dress is a cheap copy of the original that Marj wears, serves to emphasise the difference in their social status. Barbara is constantly on the defensive with Marj; she is aware that Marj looks down on her and considers her a second class person with no 'finish', which is symbolised by Marj picking at the loose thread on Barbara's dress. This loose thread can also be seen to illustrate that Marj has an unerring ability to locate Barbara's weak spots and hone in on her vulnerability.

We discover that Verge (Virginia) is Barbara's daughter who lives in an institution of some kind and that despite her claims to the contrary Marj does talk about (p. 28), criticise (p. 30) and blame (p. 27) Barbara for not being a full-time mother to Verge. Notwithstanding the fact that Barbara has been sending money every week to cover Verge's needs, Marj treats Barbara as if she has shirked her responsibility to Verge entirely. She emphasises the fact that it is Marj (her aunt) and not Barbara (her mother) who is teaching Verge 'the basics': shaving, how to catch trains and buses, and even when to clap at the symphony (p. 30). The inference is that she (Marj) would make a far better mother than Barbara has proved herself to be.

Marj patronises Barbara, making it clear that she has a need to be in control of other people — her work for the priests illustrates this. Barbara is keenly aware of Marj's feelings of superiority and attempts to undermine her attempts at control by refusing to show her their number. It is also clear that Marj enjoys her connection with the presbytery largely because of the air of genteel respectability it bestows on her. Again, Barbara tries to shake up Marj's smug complacency by suggesting that she has sex with the priests she looks after.

First Impressions of Marj

Marj is not a very likeable character. In spite of her connection with the church she exhibits some rather unchristian traits: she is self-righteous, a snob, and insensitive. She appears to enjoy feeling superior to Barbara and 'puts her down' as often as she can — 'You should have let me take you to a proper restaurant' (p. 28), 'We're lucky one of us has a home' (p. 30), 'This is not a colour I'd ever pick for you' (p. 31), 'Mummy said it. Daddy said it. You're nothing but a drifter' (p. 32). Displaying a singular lack of insight, Marj attributes Barbara's resentment towards her to the fact that Barbara did not 'inherit' their mother's earrings. Marj demonstrates not only her lack of understanding of Barbara's situation but also her own materialistic and childish nature.

Scene 11 (p. 33)

With her suitcases loaded up in a shopping trolley, Verge delivers the monologue about the two little sisters in the lake.

Verge's Story

Verge's story about the attempted drowning of one sister by the other is an effective way of introducing her to the audience. From the way she speaks it is clear that her intellectual capacity is below average but it is certainly not impaired to the extent that her perception of people and situations is hampered.

Significance of the Story

The story tells us several things. Barbara and Marj do not have an adult relationship. They have not grown out of their childhood rivalry and they still fight about wrongs and hurts from their past. For instance, only 'last Christmas' (p. 33) Verge heard them quarrelling over who was to blame for the incident in the lake. Verge is astute enough to understand the importance of this story she is 'forbidden to talk about' (p. 33) in that it sets out perfectly the dilemma she faces as the object of the sisters' present dispute. Her rhetorical question to the audience, 'So if your number came up, which one would you rather be in the water with...' (p. 33) highlights the two choices Verge has before her: life with financially secure, moralistic, responsible, controlling Marj or, life with unrealistic, spontaneous and naively optimistic Barbara.

The story can also be interpreted as a metaphor for the sisters' childhood and adolescence: who stood on whose shoulders and kept the other down?

Did Marj raise herself up in her parents' eyes at Barbara's expense — 'struggle up on her shoulders' (p. 33) — by showing up Barbara's non-conformist ways — her tendency to walk 'out a bit too far' (p. 33)? Or was Marj held down by Barbara whose 'drifter' (p. 32) ways limited her experience of the world because she believed she had to be extra good in order to make up for her parents' disappointment with Barbara?

Scene 12 (pp. 33 — 35)

Ron is confronted at the Works with the noose.

The noose is absolute evidence that the employees at the Works distrust Ron's 'consultancy' role — the suggestion is that they actually see him as a hangman or executioner hired by management to get rid of them.

Ron is a bit disillusioned by the opposition from the workers, and quite angry. He is blinded by his perception of himself as their saviour and tends to take the incident as a personal insult. He cannot see that he has failed to supply the men with the basic information necessary to an understanding of this huge change in their lives. Den, on the other hand, is very aware of the reasons why the workers are suspicious and Ron is frustrated by Den's sympathetic attitude towards them. Den defines their worries about having to 'skill down — losing conditions' (p. 34) and explains how new concepts like 'multi-skilling' are 'a bit confusing' (p. 35). Plainly, Ron does not have a clue about what is fundamentally important to these men and, despite his origins, he can no longer identify with 'the workers'. His 'cause-effect diagram sessions' (p. 34) are useless in the face of their fears about job and financial security and his attitude is characteristic of those people in positions of power who oversimplify economic and industrial problems by leaving out the human element.

Scene 13 (pp. 35 — 38)

Barbara moves into Den's house. This scene draws attention to the human tendency to embrace illusions.

Den's Generosity

Den has been busy preparing the house for Barbara: he has built a fence to block out the view of the steelworks she dislikes so much and he has bought champagne and silk roses to provide a romantic atmosphere. Barbara is optimistic about her 'brand new start' (p. 35) although the luggage Den carries in for her consists of a beauty case and a garbage bag. This suggests that in this house she will not only be embracing her future (the beauty case) but will also have to deal with stuff from her past (the garbage bag). Not only is Den providing Barbara with a home and the fees for her course at the Academy, it would also appear that he has agreed to support her financially, as we learn that she has 'left work' (p. 37). This serves to reinforce our impression of Den as a generous and caring person who, unlike the other adults in the play, is sensitive to the needs of others.

Barbara's Selfishness

In contrast to Den's desire to please, Barbara's selfishness is fully revealed in this scene when she throws a tantrum in order to get a room to have to herself to study in. The suspicion is raised that although Den may be motivated by love, Barbara appears to be moving in with him as a matter of convenience. This attitude causes the audience to lose some sympathy for Barbara and we realise that she has more 'genuine obstacles' to overcome in the process of her reinvention at the Academy than merely being 'short...twice as old as everyone else, and three times as fat' (p. 37).

The silk Roses and Den's Poem

The silk roses can be seen to represent the situation between Den and Barbara. Love is often symbolised by the rose, and in using silk or 'manufactured' roses, Thomson is alerting us to the fact that this relationship has come about not through 'natural' love but has been manufactured or made, through need. Barbara needs Den for financial support and material comfort, and Den needs to believe that Barbara loves him.

Den's poem (p. 30) describes the illusion shared by many characters in this play that unlikely or unexpected things will come about if you want them badly enough and have faith, regardless of any unfavourable circumstances.

Scene 14 (pp. 38 — 40)

Den attends his public speaking class and tells the story of his father's last day at the colliery.

Den relates, with more confidence than we have seen so far, a story about his father, which he finds amusing and which, interestingly, the rest of the class does not find funny. The story, which describes Den's father falling down from a stroke because the colliery manager expressed his appreciation of the good job he had done during his service at the mine, indicates that for many workers it was an accepted fact that their work was not highly valued. That Den's classmates cannot see the humour suggests either that attitudes have changed or, perhaps, that Den's audience of 'mostly estate agents and bank clerks' (p. 19) — 'white-collar' workers — experience different attitudes in the workplace from those of the 'blue-collar' variety. Through this story we also see that Den's hard and unchanging working life is not so much due to a lack of ambition as it is to a lack of expectations: he has grown up surrounded by 'mines...and small lives...' (p. 40).

Scene 15 (pp. 40 — 46)

Verge arrives at Den's and against Barbara's wishes, moves back into her mother's life. In this scene, Verge clears up the question of her 'disability'.

In this scene Den again proves that he has a better grasp of what is required in certain situations than those around him. Despite the fact that Barbara berates him as if he is the one who is the incompetent in the drawing exercise, it is clear that she really does not know what she must communicate in order to achieve the task. We are reminded of the fact that it was 'unskilled' Den (in scene 12) who demonstrated that he understood what it was that the workers needed to hear, rather than the more highly qualified Ron. We can also see that Barbara is becoming disillusioned with the Academy, and there is a sense that she is beginning to feel that her dreams for the future may not be as achievable as she initially believed.

Verge's Mild Disability

Describing herself as being 'a bit slow, maybe...' (p. 46) we can see by the way she has rebelled against her institutionalisation and by the way she handles her mother that her disability is very mild and that she has conquered her compulsion for self-mutilation. Nevertheless, Barbara is appalled that Verge has tracked her down and arrived at such a 'crucial stage' (p. 45) in her life. She tries very hard to convince Verge to return to her hostel or to go and live with Marj and the 'fluffy animals' (p. 44). Verge, through dogged persistence and Den's intervention, achieves her goal, and the scene, and Act 1, close with Verge and Den setting off to locate some blankets for her. Den's responsiveness to Verge and her need for security show the audience that he is indeed a kind and caring man. In contrast, Barbara's reaction — being so unnerved by her daughter's presence that she has ' to get some smokes' (p. 46) — makes us think that perhaps Verge's history of self-mutilation is the result of her mother's self-absorption. We see that she has been suffering from a lack of attention all her life, rather than a psychological condition.

Act Two

Scene 1 (pp. 48 — 49)

Ron and Den are fishing at the point; their different values and a hint of Ron's uncertainty about work.

As the scene opens Den is searching for Ron's watch. Den is concerned about the watch, referring to it as 'a good watch', but Ron is of the opinion that it is 'a cheap watch' (p. 48) and not a serious loss. This draws our attention to their differing sense of values and sharpens our perception of the change in Den's and Ron's attitudes: a note of uncertainty has crept into Ron's yet, in contrast, Den seems to be more positive in his outlook about work than he has ever been.

Obviously things at the Works are not turning out the way Ron expected. Where earlier in the play he was urging Den to be more dynamic and to exercise his own initiative at work, Ron is now advising caution: 'Don't hold things up — not any more than is necessary' (p. 49). Understandably concerned about his retraining, Den nevertheless allows Ron to reassure him that the 'go easy' (p. 49) policy is a temporary thing. However, the audience is aware that Ron is not being totally honest with Den and is not speaking plainly enough. He sees that he is, in fact, being used as a 'hatchet man' so that the Works can be closed down and sold off with a minimum of fuss, but he does nothing to make Den fully realise the implications of the new developments.

Scene 2 (pp. 49 — 51)

In this exchange between Den and Verge, we are exposed to the idea that wanting something is not a sufficient means to achieve it.

In the discussion between Den and Verge about dreams, the audience is being asked to compare the unrealistic dreams of the adults with Verge's dreams. Is Barbara aspiring to a hostessing job at the new resort, or Marj's wish to be Verge's substitute mother, or Ron's belief that democracy and profitability can coexist in the workplace, very much different from Verge's dreams of 'being a disco-dancer' or 'Torville and Dean' (p. 50)? Den tells Verge to 'just be here' (p. 51), signalling that the important thing in life is who you are and not what you do. The closeness between

Den and Verge is very apparent in this scene. Even when Den responds to Verge's declaration of love with 'You've been watching too much television' (p. 51) as Barbara did in Act 1 scene 15 (p. 45) we can tell that Den says it with genuine affection.

Scene 3 (p. 51)

Ron is moving out of the Works site.

The fact that Ron is relocating to offices in the city is significant. His vague explanation about 'Paperwork' (p. 51) leaves us with a sense that things are being 'wrapped up' and that the end for the Works is not far off. Ron's departure from Den's workplace heralds his intrusion into Den's home: Jeannie, whom Den has continued to avoid contacting, is obviously intent on selling the house and has asked Ron to look it over in preparation for getting it valued. Coming as this scene does after Verge and Den's discussion about dreams, we have to question whether it is only large, ambitious dreams that are unrealistic or is it the case that for some, dreams of any kind — even simple ones — are foolish. All Den was looking for was a partner, a happy home life and an income that would allow him to achieve his modest dream, but the outlook for his future at this point looks very grim indeed.

Scene 4 (pp. 51 — 55)

Den and Barbara explore the almost finished Resort hotel.

The muzak version of The Beatles' song 'The Fool on the Hill' that runs through this scene like a reprise, underscores the air of hopelessness surrounding the future for Barbara and Den.

Whilst Barbara is impressed by the fact that even an unfinished hotel can be so 'classy' as to have muzak playing, the audience sees this 'counterfeit' music as further evidence that the hotel is merely another crassly commercial and poor quality business venture that is bound to upset the quality of life in the area.

Barbara's Responses to the Hotel

The hotel acts on Barbara like an aphrodisiac: her desire to be a part of it translates into a physical desire for Den. This is significant because we can see that if it wasn't for the promise of a successful future for herself that she saw in the resort project, it is unlikely that she would have moved in with Den or even had a relationship with him. Den's patronage enabled her to leave work and pay for her full-time study at the Academy, and her mercenary side is further highlighted when she reminds him that 'the next instalment of fees are due' (p. 55). Although she insists that she is 'worth it' (p. 55) we cannot help but wonder.

Den sees Barbara's limitations

Den is unimpressed by the hotel, probably because he can see it for what it is. He is certainly realistic in his vision of the part Barbara would be most likely to play in the operation. In reassuring her that he would not 'let them give [her] a cleaning job' (p. 54), he voices what the audience has realised all along. No amount of grooming, elocution or deportment will change Barbara into the sort of person an organisation like that would allow to have contact with its guests. Regardless of how Den tries to distract Barbara from her fantasy of the hotel — the picnic, the umbrella, 'you haven't got the job yet' (p. 52) — like a besotted lover she appears to remain deliberately blind to the real world around her.

Scene 5 (pp. 55 — 58)

Den and Verge are on the hill watching the birds. Verge is blossoming in the family environment that Den has created for her; clearly, the two of them derive a lot of pleasure from one another's company.

By engaging Den in the discussion of the birds, Verge is able to indirectly gain the reassurance she needs that her place in the family is secure. Her question to Den about the baby shows that they both share the ideal of 'family', unlike Barbara whose focus for fulfilment in life lies, as we know, elsewhere.

Bearing in mind Barbara's obsession with the hotel that has been so graphically portrayed in the previous scene, Verge's acute awareness of the difference between fact and fantasy is demonstrated through the 'make-believe' she and Den share about the migratory birds.

> DEN: You know you were looking at pigeons up there.
>
> VERGE: Yes. I knew. (p. 58)

This serves to emphasise Barbara's lack of ability to see things as they really are.

The Poem — 'Cargoes'

Thomson uses John Masefield's poem 'Cargoes' here as a way of drawing together the ideas and ideals that we have been exposed to so far. The stanzas quoted in this scene romanticise industry and trade through the listing of unusual foreign names and places and the rich, exotic cargoes;

they also work as a metaphor for the grand quality of the dreams and visions for their lives that the different characters have revealed.

Scene 6 (pp. 58 — 65)

Barbara and Den are hosting a party. Ron, their invited guest, spends a rather long time crawling around under the house inspecting the foundations whilst Marj, their 'uninvited' guest finds herself the centre of attention as she wrangles with Barbara over Verge's refusal to accompany her on a weekend away.

There are plenty of comic (even 'slap-stick') elements included in this scene, such as the garish, flashing lights, the 'flying' savouries, Verge responding to Marj's arrival by shutting the door in her face and leaving her on the doorstep, and the erratic intrusions of the music. Nevertheless, a pathetic note of sadness underlies the action.

Barbara unaware of impending loss

Barbara is 'holding court' by herself because Ron, the 'guest of honour', is under the house performing a pre-sale inspection. The home that Barbara is so proudly talking about — 'my head's full of plans for this place' (p. 60) — whilst not in danger of 'sliding down the hill' (p. 59), is, in any event, going to 'slide' out from underneath her. Unbeknownst to her and on Jeannie's orders, it is about to be sold.

Barbara's attempt to thank Ron for what he has done for Den and his employment prospects is sadly ironic because we know that all he has actually achieved is Den's future unemployment. Barbara's attempt to pass herself off as a member of a public relations agency is certainly amusing on the surface, but the lack of self-worth and quiet desperation that this ruse illuminates again undermines the comical side. Her pathetic attempts at 'sophistication' are more sad than funny, especially when we realise that the hotel is about to open and she has not even managed to get an interview.

Ron's Character

This scene also confirms that Ron is indeed, a joke, although there is little that we can find amusing about him. He shows himself to be not only a moral coward, but disloyal and self-interested too. He is joining in with Den and Barbara's celebrations under false pretences, because even though he knows exactly what is going on, he neither makes clear Jeannie's plans to make Den homeless, nor the Department's plans to make him jobless as well. Even without 'inside information' he manages to tarnish Barbara's illusions about the resort hotel (p. 60). However, with her uncanny ability to see right into the heart of a person, Verge does not hesitate to expose Ron's insincere nature when he pretends to know more than he really does: 'Ron. Bullshit you know Kelvin Pearce' (p 61). Amongst all the pretence in this scene, Verge's plain speaking and distaste for 'bullshit' is refreshing.

Marj's humiliation and Den's avoidance of facts

Nevertheless, even Verge is not totally innocent of guile. We cannot help but suspect that she has accepted Marj's offer to go away for the weekend with the ulterior motive of forcing Marj to visit the 'family' home. Verge wants Marj to see that the home is nice, that Barbara is successful, 'Mum graduated and her photo was in the paper' (p. 63) and that she is loved and does not need Marj's thin substitute affection. When faced with Barbara, Den and Verge as a united family unit, Marj is humiliated, loses her composure, and shows herself to be the type of person who does 'good works' in order to promote herself in the eyes of others. Neither of the sisters appears to want to face reality — either about themselves, or the lives they live.

Den too, shows that he has a preference for avoiding facts. He knows he should question Ron further about what his firm's role actually is now that it has gone into the 'getting a report out' (p. 65) phase. However, we sense that fear of the truth keeps him from extracting the information from Ron.

Scene 7 (p. 65)

Verge and Den take down the party lights and recite the third stanza of their poem. From this point on the mood of the play becomes one of disintegration and lost illusions.

This interlude confirms for the audience that the party is certainly over, in more ways than one. The stanza of Masefield's poem that Den and Verge recite is analogous to the reality of what is happening. Gone are the references to the foreign and exotic. The 'Stately Spanish galleon' (p. 58) has been replaced by a 'Dirty *British* coaster' (p. 65). The rich and romantic cargoes have been replaced by utilitarian and unattractive ones containing 'coal', 'road rail', 'pig-lead', 'firewood' and 'iron-ware' (p. 65), all things that can be linked with the necessities and mundanities of life in an industrial town — the reality of *their* lives. Under the circumstances it is ironically fitting that Thomson gives the line 'cheap tin-trays' (p. 65) to Ron as he slinks from the stage: his character, behaviour and expertise, as we have witnessed, are a far cry from the real thing.

Scene 8 (p. 66)

In his final public speaking class, Den relates the story of his father's experience as a prisoner during World War II.

Significance of the Burma Railway story

Den's confidence when speaking in public has vastly improved. He is confident and articulate. The story he tells of the 'mythical' Japanese hospital supposedly available for the incapacitated men of the infamous Burma Railway, is a shocking reminder of the ruthlessness that mankind is capable of when the success of a project relies solely on expediency. Thomson is asking the audience to make the connection between the sacrifice of 'the sickest fifty men' (p. 66) and Ron's admission in Act 2, scene 1, that he had been asked 'to target another fifty. To go' (p. 48). It is a little unsettling to realise that Den's first instinct was to let the 'blokes on light duties' (p. 49) go, even despite the fact that his intention was to stop 'their injuries get[ting] worse' (p. 48). In reality we have to question whether there would have been much difference in the fate of these men laid off work due to their injuries and that of the abandoned, chronically ill prisoners — at least while they worked, both groups were in possession of the 'means' to eat.

Importance of the story to Den

A further correspondence to be found in this story is that, like his father before him, Den had doubts about the practicality of all the plans for the rejuvenation of the Works, and again like his father, he did not speak out about his fears. Instead, he allowed himself to be talked out of them by Ron. This story is important to Den because the experience was a turning point for his father. It was the last time he quietly acceded to the ideas of those in authority: 'After that he became a man who always spoke his mind' (p. 66). This story also foreshadows the stand Den takes at the end of the play.

Scene 9 (pp. 67- 69)

Barbara tries hard to convince Den to send Verge away. Den finally tells Barbara that the house they are living in does not belong to him, but is owned by his sister Jeannie.

Barbara's responses to possible failure

Barbara is not coping at all well emotionally — she is devastated that she has not had any success in gaining an interview at the new resort. From her account of the conversation she had with the Academy, and Den's consternation about what Barbara is wearing, we know that no matter how hard she tries she is never going to make the grade. We suspect that deep down she knows this too and as a consequence is resorting to playing the lottery as her last hope of ever changing her life.

Barbara's selfishness and lack of maternal ability show through in her belief that Verge is the reason that things are going wrong for her. She sees her daughter as a blight on her chances for a bright future, and blames the tension between herself and Den on Verge's presence. Under the circumstances it is no surprise that Barbara is 'somewhat horrified' (p. 68) by Den's allusion to a child of their own. She also fails to show any understanding of the worries that Den is faced with in light of the 'rumours flying around work' (p. 67) and his financial responsibility for the three of them. Once again she shows that Den is not her primary consideration and she rebukes him for suggesting that they go to bed at five o'clock in the afternoon something which, she says, 'Only very common people' do (p. 69).

Den's responses

It is interesting to note that Barbara's reaction to the disintegration of her dreams is to break up the family unit by sending Verge away, whereas Den's is to attempt to tie it together more strongly and even add to it with a baby of their own.

Scene 10 (pp. 69-72)

Ron tells Den that the Works are going to be closed down and sold.

Ron finally comes clean with Den and exposes the deception that has been perpetrated with regard to the fate of the steelworks. Den takes an agonisingly long time to fully grasp what Ron is telling him which is hardly surprising when we consider that he has had his heart set on his welder's ticket and now, suddenly, he has to face the fact that it is not going to happen. Ron is at pains to distance himself from the decision-making process that has brought this about, explaining that the Government had really already decided the outcome beforehand. When we look at the 'selling off' process, we can see that at the end of the day the major players will all be able to justify their actions and walk away with clear consciences. We see that Ron's firm was used as 'window dressing'; the government has made a legitimate sale to private enterprise; Davis and Dixon (the purchasers) in order to safeguard their investment will make an economically sound decision and legitimately dispose of the asset for a profit. Typically, it is only the 'little men' — the workers — who will gain nothing but hardship from the actions of those who are bigger and more powerful.

Unable to comprehend the damage he has done in raising Den's hopes and abusing his trust, Ron is desperate to ensure that Den will accept the payout that will be offered, but Den is bitterly disappointed and resentful and is in no mood to be 'bought off'.

Scene 11 (pp. 72-75)

Barbara is elated over Den's redundancy payout even though he still appears adamant that he will not accept it.

From her excited behaviour, the audience could be forgiven for thinking, initially, that Barbara had finally won the lottery. Even the words of praise she has for Den are, perhaps, more appropriate to a lucky ticket: 'I knew you. I had you spotted. I knew you'd come up with something' (p. 73), rather than a man who has just been condemned to the unemployment line for the rest of his life. Barbara has no conception of the long-term impact that Den's termination will have on the household's economy. As she seems unable to look past the 'bloody thousands' (p. 73) she imagines Den is getting, she fails to realise that Den is being pushed out the door after all his years of service with not 'even a year's wages' (p. 73).

Her impracticality and self-centredness are brought sharply into focus. When Den asks Barbara, 'Tell me who I am. What you see?' (p. 74) she does not catch on that for Den, losing his job means losing his purpose in life as well as a vital part of his identity. Barbara has no time for the people around her because she is totally focused on achieving her new goal of a beach equipment hire service. Den and Verge only make her impatient because they are 'in the way': Den because he does not want to take the money, and Verge because she is physically present and wants to be a part of Den and Barbara's discussion. As the scene progresses Barbara becomes more desperate to get her way, until finally she is even prepared to try and sway Den with a bribe about having a baby, something which we know she has no desire to do.

Sadly, Den is starting to realise that all along Barbara's priority in their relationship has been money rather than love. His worth was in what he could do for her,

> ***not who he was — he was a means to an end; a way to achieve the lifestyle she craved.***

Den is beginning to see that no-one really cares how much potential he has for self-improvement, whether that improvement means effectively embracing the new work practices or by grasping the techniques of public speaking. He is being harshly shown that his 'dollar' value is more important than his value as a worthwhile human being. It is also unfortunate that because of the prompting he received from Ron and Barbara to change his ways, Den no longer believes in lying down and taking injustice quietly as he used to. He now has too much self-respect to be blatantly bought off and leave 'on tip-toes' (p. 75). Den has been shaken out of his state of apathy to become a man of principles and ironically, it has happened at the time in his life when it will do him the least good.

Scene 12 (pp. 76-78)

Ron confronts Den about his determination to refuse the payout.

There is little doubt that Ron's conscience is the primary motivator in his efforts to convince Den to take the money: 'You see I won't let you do this to me. I will not have you on my conscience' (p. 76). Ron's sense of guilt is understandable as he knows he has been instrumental in Den's loss of employment and the newly acquired assertiveness that is causing him to sacrifice everything by taking such a futile stand. When Den gets an inkling of what Ron has put in his report, 'touchy, moody, badly organised work force' (p. 76), Den's contempt for Ron and his job boil over. Den tells Ron that his (Ron's) job is 'a racket' (p. 77) because, at the end of the day, those reports merely state the obvious and why things cannot be rectified rather than how they could be. He is also resentful that there is never an element of risk for people like Ron.

> DEN: You don't take risks, you're like the person on the beach who sees someone in a rip, takes his shoes off, jumps up and down and hopes he looks like he's about to dive in (p. 77).

Ron misinterprets 'You look after your own light'

If we were in any doubt that it is people like Den in this world who enable others to achieve, the actions of Ron and Jeannie remove any traces. Thomson shows us that Den and the blue-collar work force to which he belongs contribute substantially to a profit-making process from which they never benefit. When the government's potential profits from the steelworks were seen to be greater if they sold it than if they continued to run it as an industry, the decision was not a difficult one to make: the men's livelihoods were sacrificed. On a smaller scale we can see that Ron and Jeannie sacrifice Den in much the same way. Having helped Ron become qualified, Den falls victim to the 'recommendations' of Ron and his firm in the workplace. Unfortunately, too, because Ron has advance warning of what is about to happen in the town, the profit Jeannie will make from getting the family home Den has been living in on the market 'quickly before the rest of the street does' (p. 78), will be increased.

Ron encapsulates the creed of 'every man for himself' by which the more powerful members of society operate when he says, 'you look after your own light' (p. 78). Ironically, however, he has misunderstood that what was meant by this saying in the mines, where a strong team ethic was vitally important to everyone's safety, was that you took responsibility for yourself so as not to put the rest of the team at risk. It is not surprising that Ron missed the point.

Scene 13 (pp. 78-83)

It is show-down time. Barbara has made up her mind that she will not stay with Den and she vents her anger and resentment at his decision to refuse the redundancy money. Den finally sees her for what she is and not what he imagined her to be — especially when Verge emerges bound and gagged from the cupboard.

With her hopes and dreams in tatters — like the panty-hose she fruitlessly sorts through — Barbara is at her wits' end. Her fantasy of being a refined, sophisticated and successful woman has been destroyed by the Resort Hotel's lack of interest in her and Den's refusal of the money. This double-bind restricts her in much the same way as the double-gusset would if she used Den's solution to her panty-hose problem: 'You wear a double-gusset and see how relaxed you feel' (p. 79). Incredibly, she is getting ready to go and confront the hotel management and demand her chance for an interview.

Den, who has been watching her deteriorate, is not prepared to allow her to make a fool of herself, even though he realises that she no longer cares for him. Barbara is in no mood to listen to home-truths and retaliates to Den's hurtful but honest observations with venom, spite and sexual innuendo. At this point it would be easy for us to say that in losing

Barbara, Den has not really lost all that much because she never really loved him anyway. But to do this would be to subscribe to the kind of thinking used by those people who push for industrial reform without considering the impact on the people whose lives are directly affected. Barbara, although flawed in our eyes, was who Den wanted and needed to give him emotional fulfilment and a sense of family, just as his labourer's job at the Works, although boring and not very satisfying, gave him financial independence and a sense of purpose.

The last straw for Den is not only Barbara's act of tying Verge up and shutting her in a cupboard, but also her vile suggestion that he has been sexually involved with Verge. To his credit, he realises that Barbara is lashing out in the only way she knows because she is hurt, angry and disillusioned and is incapable of recognising — let alone admitting — the part she has played in her own demise. We could say that the relationship between Barbara and Den was doomed from the beginning mainly because they occupied opposite sides of life's 'quality/quantity' formula.

Scene 14 (pp. 83-86)

Den makes his stand at the Works.

In this scene we witness the futility of Den's noble act of self-sacrifice on behalf of his fellow workers. The real tragedy of Den's refusal to accept the payout or re-deployment is that no-one cares.

Neither management nor his colleagues are interested or affected by what Den has done or by what he has to say. In fact, it is only the threat that Den will set himself alight and as a consequence probably set fire to the whole factory, that causes the men to shut their machines down and let him be heard. The points Den makes in attempting to expose the outrageously callous treatment of the workers by the government, although expressed in simple, straightforward language, are valid and astute. Arguably, it is the very simplicity with which Den expresses himself that gives what he has to say even more impact — for the audience at least.

Den has paid a high price for his desire to be a man of principle and 'speak his mind'. He will suffer great personal hardship from passing up the chance of another, albeit menial, job as well as forfeiting the redundancy package that would have provided him with some very necessary financial assistance. This is not appreciated by the other men whose apathetic acceptance of what has happened indicates that they have either been re-deployed or believe that this kind of thing is merely their 'lot' in life.

Verge's despairing response

However, it is in Verge that we find the most graphic depiction of the consequences of the type of closure that the Works has undergone. Simple, innocent Verge is the symbol of those who are sacrificed by the accountants and the economic rationalists in the name of efficiency, modernity and profit. In the face of the effect that the events at the Works in this scene have on Verge, Den's stand with his 'fake' petrol can appears hollow and a bit foolish. It is Verge, the most helpless member of this little community that can be seen to pay the highest price, as her blood spills from the wounds she inflicts on herself in her despair. Ultimately, she is the one chosen by Thomson to truly represent the plight of the workers.

Scene 15 (pp. 86-87)

Barbara and Den meet for the last time. The significance of the play's title is revealed.

Thomson does justice to the serious themes and issues addressed in this work by not diluting their grim and confronting aspects with a 'happy ending'. The air of uncertainty that surrounds the contemporary workplace arises from an abiding ethic of 'profit before people', Thomson reveals the all-too-often hidden, personal aspect of the difficulties faced by a broad cross-section of people in Australian society who are just trying to 'get by'.

Farewell to Barbara and Den

In this final scene, we find ourselves saying goodbye to Den and Barbara on the same hill where we first met them — we have come full circle. This is a much calmer encounter than when we last saw them together (Act 2, pp. 78-83) and there is a sense that any animosity they may have harboured towards one another has become insignificant in comparison to the personal defeat that each has suffered. Barbara has returned to her brittle, cynical self and Den has little to say — which is not surprising given that he has no job, no home and no family. In these rather bleak circumstances it is pleasing to discover that Den intends to maintain his relationship with Verge and that he will do so with Marj's approval.

Marj

It would appear that Marj has also recognised the importance of putting the needs of others before her own. Barbara, although obviously not likely to elect to share her life with Verge, shows that she is still interested in her daughter's welfare, a fact that tends to make the audience a little more forgiving towards her. We are able to realise, as Den did, that Barbara too, is a victim of the circumstances that have surrounded her life.

Diving for Pearls

The little story Barbara tells about the boys diving off the wharf for silver coins and sometimes being tricked into taking the risk and putting in the effort for a relatively worthless 'dirty old' (p. 87) penny, illustrates what she and Den have been doing throughout the play. The 'pearls' that Barbara was diving for were social respectability, refinement, and financial success, whilst Den's were the 'pearls' of love, family and personal and professional fulfilment. The tragedy is, of course, that they have had to work so hard in order to survive, let alone improve themselves, that the opportunity for them to gather riches and pearls has passed them by. This, in turn, invites the speculation that perhaps Thomson is also reminding us that through not respecting and appreciating one another, we run the risk of missing out on the most valuable pearls of all.

Den

> DEN: I told you what I'm like — a quiet corner with a cowboy novel and a couple of devon sandwiches (p. 3).

There was a popular saying during the late 1980s and early 1990s to the effect that 'nice guys come last'. Arguably, Den is the personification of this saying. In direct contrast to 'Texan Ted' who, we are told, 'never fails to win. And...always gets the girl on the last page' (p. 17), we see Den progressively lose everything until, in the last scene of the play, we watch with him as Barbara walks out of his life. A quiet, unassuming man with 'old-fashioned' values, Den is not suited to the intrigues and 'hidden agendas' inherent in a lifestyle geared exclusively to the material success of the individual. For him life is all about team-work: couples, families, workers all giving their best for a common good rather than a personal triumph. Den is the 'nice guy' who, never having an ulterior motive when dealing with others himself, cannot recognise when others are taking advantage of him.

Den becomes a casualty of the ambitions of others. Ron eventually sacrifices him for the success of his project and to satisfy Jeannie's desire to profit from the sale of the house; Barbara deserts him when the money and the prospects run out; his employer, the government, abandons him in favour of a quick, healthy profit. It is perhaps this last 'sell-out' that is the worst blow of all for Den because work is an intrinsically important part of who he is as a person, and the pride he takes in doing even a relatively menial job well is patently obvious. Although he could be accused of lacking ambition, this can be attributed more to his view of himself as a member of a team than to any laziness on his part, because when he finally succumbs to Ron's persuasion he is extremely keen to improve himself and get his welder's ticket.

Thomson's portrayal of Den as a decent man is a subtle one drawn mainly through his fair and honest dealings with others. He is generous to Barbara; he willingly protects and nurtures Verge whilst maintaining straightforward communication with her, quietly persisting in the face of Marj's interference and disapproval. He is loyal to both his employer and his co-workers. These qualities all demonstrate his strength of character, making what happens to him in the play all the more unacceptable to the audience. We respect that Den is a man of principle and that he does not stir up trouble for its own sake. Consequently, his decision to take a stand against the callous disloyalty of 'the bosses' by refusing the inadequate redundancy package and speaking out on the factory floor to his fellow workers, although ultimately ineffective, carries substantial moral weight. Perhaps Thomson is suggesting that by not speaking out people actually become complicit in such heartless treatment of one another.

Barbara

> BARBARA: ...Never ever in my entire life has the right thing happened at the right time. True. I've always been patting a flying bird. Well, we'll catch it this time, even if we have to whack it on the head with a hammer (p. 73).

Despite the fact that she is selfish, coarse and unrealistic, Barbara is not a totally unsympathetic character. Her optimism and fearless determination to do whatever it takes to achieve her goals, although far from subtle, are qualities which an audience recognises and admires. Barbara has never had the right 'breaks' — there has always been something preventing her from fulfilling her potential. Her life has been hard and we can see that it has hardened her; it is possibly because of this that she is so insensitive in her dealings with other people and so unaware of her own shortcomings. On the surface it should be easy for us to find Barbara ridiculous when she attempts to reinvent herself as a lady of 'quality'. However, it is the pathetic hopelessness of her mission that invites our sympathy. Barbara has been thinking 'about money pretty solidly for most of [her] waking life' (p. 73) and in her mind it has become the answer to happiness and fulfilment. It is clear that her obsession with material gain has dulled her ability to appreciate the less tangible but far more important values of life like love, family, honesty and loyalty. Barbara's belief in simple pleasures has been lost in her pursuit of money and sophistication.

However, her treatment of Verge is difficult to forgive, even despite the fact that Verge's disability makes her a rather hefty responsibility. It is not in Barbara's favour that even with the stable home environment that Den provides she is still unwilling to be a mother to Verge, she continually attempts to escape from her despite the fact that we recognise how trying Verge's behaviour and inappropriate remarks must be. The desperation inherent in Barbara's cruel act of tying Verge up, gagging her, and locking her in the cupboard clearly shows how incapable of she is of being a parent. This is in stark contrast to Den's success with Verge thanks to his ability to effectively communicate with her and to foster mutual understanding. We can see that Barbara's approach to dealing with the world is indeed to 'whack it on the head with a hammer' (p. 73).

Ron

> RON: I'm a junkie for all this. Still a hoon. I mean, is that it or is that it? (p. 10).

> RON: I'm smirked at by every conscientious young prick who's ever walked in the door of my firm, because my degree's not posh enough (p. 76).

> RON: ...You don't just hold on. When the ground's cracking from under you, you predict where the crevices'll appear and leap onto the next safe patch. Stand there gaping and you're on your own without any water (p. 77).

Ron becomes increasingly less likeable as the play progresses. At first we can see through his 'hoon' act to the rather insecure 'local boy made good' underneath. When he remarks to Den, 'I keep thinking I'll come face to face with myself coming around a corner. A twenty-year-old hoon' (p. 9) it is clear that he has not quite made the transition in his own mind from his labourer days at the Works to his professional role in the consultancy. He makes no secret of the fact that his colleagues in the consultancy consider his qualifications to be a bit second-rate and we can see that he does not share Jeannie's pretensions: 'Couldn't get out of Perth quick enough. Cowboys and wankers...[Jeannie's] right at home in Perth' (p. 9). His initial desire to facilitate the financial turn-around of the Works appears to be genuine — probably because he would not only increase in status in the eyes of his colleagues but also because it would make him a bit of a hero in his old home town.

He seems to be powerless in his marriage with Jeannie, 'Hasn't changed, your sister. Still only does exactly what suits her' (p. 8) and this can be seen to parallel his ultimate powerlessness professionally. Just as he capitulates and falls in with Jeannie's plans to sell the house, so he gives in and ends up writing the kind of report that the government wants. Ron's ability to save himself at the expense of others can be explained in two ways. Firstly, he becomes representative of the ruthless and greedy face of economic rationalism and those who 'serve' it. Secondly, he also demonstrates how a weak individual who is unsure of where he really belongs is compelled to keep on the right side of those people perceived to be the holders of power.

Nevertheless, Ron is a ruthless survivor who does not let his heart get in the way of his head. In his own way he is as careless with the lives and well-being of the employees at the Works, as evidenced in his manipulation of Den, as the government bosses in control at the top. He does not even have the courage to be straight with Den and lay out all the facts, which makes his ultimate act of blaming Den for 'shooting [himself] in the arse' (p. 76) utterly unforgivable.

Marj

> MARJ: I only want to know if you need some help. I am your sister — why won't you return my calls? If you need help, you know I'm prepared to come down...Please remember though that the three of us can constitute a family, Barbara. Yes, it might be very sad, but we can (p. 25).
>
> MARJ: We're lucky one of us has a home she can come to (p. 30).
>
> MARJ: Dear God, I'd love to know what I've done to you...the number of times I've put myself out for you (p. 64).
>
> MARJ: It's not as if I'm asking for gratitude — (p. 65)

Even though Marj is a snob who tends to believe that there are certain types of people in the world who cannot be allowed to operate independently because they are not well enough equipped, it would be unfair to judge her too harshly. It is true that she has a tendency to control others and that she is a 'do-gooder' for whom charity is a way of demonstrating to the world, at the expense of the dignity of others, what a worthy person she is. Nevertheless she does sincerely believe that she is doing the right thing.

For all her financial independence, Marj's experience of the world appears to have been fairly limited. She is unmarried, the work she does for the parish priests is purely on a voluntary basis (she does not have to work in order to earn money), and she has not yet grown up enough to stop referring to her parents as 'Mummy' and 'Daddy' (p. 32). We can see that it has been relatively simple for Marj to maintain what she sees as her moral superiority living as she does such a circumscribed life. As Verge intimates in scene 11 (p. 33), deciding who is the more appealing of the two sisters is not a simple task. For all her lack of refinement there is something marvellously alive about Barbara. Marj, despite her genteel manners and financially secure place in society, has a rather sad and lonely life. Each woman is as determined as the other to have her own way: 'which one would you rather be in the water with…which one… (Verge, p. 33).

Verge

> VERGE: [*nearly shouting*] Well I think I must be different! (p. 45)
>
> VERGE: I just need security. It was in my file and it's true. Somewhere I belong. And no bullshit (p. 46).
>
> VERGE: I'm not stupid…A bit slow, maybe… Just a bit slow to catch on. Sparks in the brain (p. 46).

Personifying those people who are most vulnerable in our society, Verge compels us to think about the 'duty of care' that should be a major consideration in our day-to-day dealings with one another. She might be slow, but she is far from stupid, almost instinctively recognising the truly important things necessary to give quality to life. Unlike some of the other characters, Verge's life does not depend on money for its improvement and the reality of this is brought home to us when she states that 'security' and 'somewhere [to] belong' (p. 46) are what she needs most. The character least able to tolerate 'bullshit' p. 46), Verge demonstrates an uncanny ability to identify falseness and a discomforting tendency to ignore the restrictions of 'social politeness' and state the truth without hesitation.

Barbara's financial contribution to Verge's upkeep at the institution falls well short of supplying her real needs; this serves to aid our understanding of why Den's redundancy payout is so unacceptable to him. Marj's rather self-serving interest in Verge's well-being reflects the self-interest that drives Ron's and Barbara's attentions towards Den.

Under the circumstances, it is little wonder that when the haven of her newly found family is destroyed we see her old wounds re-opened as she resorts, once again, to self-mutilation.

THEMES & ISSUES

Dreams

Dreaming is a strong motif in *Diving for Pearls* and Thomson reveals how important the capacity to dream is for human beings. The play explores the many facets of 'dreaming'. We witness the 'everyday' meaning in the form of the dreams of sleep (Verge p. 50). We follow with interest characters as they pursue dreams which take the form of hopes and ambitions for the future (Barbara and Den). Eventually we find ourselves face-to-face with questions about the notion of an 'Australian Dream' and what this particular collective imagining might actually disclose.

Thomson shows us that on a personal level, dreams assist in the maintenance of individual identity and that it is through dreams that people find the stamina to persevere and keep on striving in their lives. On a national level, it is those collective dreams that capture the imagination of a culture or society giving it purpose, shape and meaning by encapsulating a consensus of values about personal and material success.

It is important to remember that while dreams can be sustaining in nature, they can also make people vulnerable; Thomson illustrates this through Barbara's exploitation at the hands of the Academy and by the way Den yields to Ron's manipulation for the sake of the opportunity to further his training. Consequently, we are faced with the unpleasant truth about people and organisations, through their management, who have no hesitation in feeding off and jeopardising the dreams of others in order to make their own lives more prosperous and secure.

Australian Myths and Realities

Thomson questions characteristics of the Australian way of life that we take for granted and which make up our 'national myth'. She asks us to look at the degree to which the value placed on work and workers, home ownership, equal opportunity, the 'classless' society and 'mateship' are actually evident in our society.

Work and Workers

Australia prides itself on being a nation of good workers and employment is seen as both a necessity and a right. Having a job is viewed not only as a way to ensure financial security and to achieve the material benefits that flow on from that security, but also to strengthen, even ensure, in some cases, personal identity and self-esteem. Accordingly, all the characters in the play are workers, and it is clear that the work they do is very much a part of who they are. Reliable Den depends on his uninspiring but vital part of the production line. Ron revels in his 'quick fix' consultancy. Marj needs the virtuous volunteer work for the priests. Barbara is frustratingly limited by piecework in the factory, and Verge in her sheltered workshop performing tasks beneath her capabilities in frightful conditions, finally rebels.

Australians attach a very real stigma to being 'on the dole' or unemployed and it is presumed that people who receive government benefits are lazy, immoral or unintelligent — effectively, 'deficient' human beings. However, Thomson illustrates just how difficult it can be to maintain the right to work. *Diving for Pearls* exposes the ruthless behaviour organisations are capable of, for example, throwing Den on the retrenchment 'scrapheap' with little hope for the future, and getting Verge 'sacked' (p. 45) because she strenuously objects to the conditions under which she and the other employees work. Thomson shows us that making assumptions about people and situations based on a national ideal rather than fact can lead not only to gross injustice but to a dangerous lack of awareness of the prevailing conditions in our society.

Home Ownership

It is taken for granted by Australians, unlike so many other people in the world, that the opportunity for home-ownership will be theirs. In fact, this right to own real estate is a major part of the 'Australian dream' and it incorporates not only the physical dwelling but the ideal of family, love and security. In Den and Barbara we see two people for whom the Australian dream is out of reach. Thomson shows us clearly that Barbara's chances for a home and family of her own are pretty slim. Since she has rejected her place for subsidised housing by walking away from the Housing Commission home she shared with her husband (p. 5), she is relegated to renting a single room in a boarding house. For many years, Den has occupied the family home alone. Now, with his ejection from it by Jeannie, which coincides with his loss of employment and his loss of Barbara, it is obvious that for him too, home ownership and all it represents will not be available in the near future.

On the other hand, it is through the examples of Marj and Ron who do own homes of their own — Ron and Jeannie actually have one each — that Thomson really shows us the flaws in the Australian dream. Marj's home is an empty one that contains no loving family, and it would appear that an abundance of homes has not given Ron domestic happiness.

With her portrayal of the good fortune for the owners of the cottages 'stuck out on...cliffs' (p. 3), Thomson illustrates the degeneration of the dream and what home ownership has come to mean. For them, like Jeannie, the family home is ultimately a piece of real estate on which profit can be made.

Equal Opportunity and the Classless Society

Another ideal which underpins the Australian national myth is that hard work rather than money or class, is the key to personal success and achievement. The notion that for every Australian there is a state of equal opportunity is shown in *Diving for Pearls* to be a fallacy. The play clearly shows us that all characters do not share the same bright prospects for the future and Thomson exposes some of the forces that work against individuals who have ambition and a desire to achieve.

We understand that Ron will never get as far in his firm as his colleagues because he has an inferior educational qualification. Den will not be redeployed because he has not had the opportunity to gain the necessary skills, and Barbara has little chance of improving her employment prospects because she lacks the education and breeding required for the jobs to which she aspires.

It is made clear that there is a division in status between Den and Barbara's city and the place where Marj lives: 'She doesn't think you're human if you live down here' (Barbara about Marj, p. 64). Further, we see that within itself, the community has become divided according to degrees of wealth. 'You could divide this city in half...They're getting everything up there.' (Barbara, p. 3) a state of affairs which reveals how economic policies can actually privilege those who are already quite well-off or powerful at the expense of the less fortunate and not so powerful: 'You're a cost and they're cutting costs. Well, bad luck. We're all servants of accountancy...' (p. 76). Employees may be sacrificed along the way, but big business will survive.

Instead of a democratic society in which, in principle at least, everyone is supposed to be equal, Thomson shows us that in fact 'money talks' and that without it you have little or no say in how your life will be run.

'Mateship'

The Australian national characteristic of 'mateship' has taken on legendary status. Representing an abiding cultural trait of loyalty and 'fair play', mateship not only encapsulates the willingness of individuals to stick together and support one another when times get tough, but also the tendency of Australians to look out for the well-being of the less fortunate members of society — the 'underdogs'.

Again, Thomson shows us a picture of reality that differs from the one we hold in our national imagination. Far from protecting his 'mate', Ron sacrifices Den both at work and at home. Although a male concept, it is perceived to be relevant to men and women alike. Barbara is cast aside by the women at the Academy when it becomes obvious that her need for assistance is substantially more than usual and Verge is exploited at the Sheltered Workshop by the very people who are supposed to be providing those in their care with special concern and attention.

Hope for the Future

Diving for Pearls shows us much of the negative aspects of human nature and society, but it can be argued that Thomson does, in fact, provide a positive side to this drama. Through Den's loving, compassionate and understanding nature and the courage and tenacity demonstrated by Barbara, Den and Verge, we can identify those human qualities that Thomson believes to be of intrinsic value. The play suggests that true wealth and happiness could be ours if we would only cultivate more honest and caring ways of dealing with each other, demonstrate courage and determination in the face of hardship and injustice, and remember the importance of the saying, 'united we stand — divided we fall'.

QUESTIONS & ANSWERS

Sample Exam Questions

1. *Diving for Pearls* is about change and the inability of some people to cope with it. Discuss.
2. Dreaming is something all people do but in *Diving for Pearls* we see what a futile enterprise dreaming really is. To what extent do you agree with this statement?
3. Barbara is not deserving of our sympathy because she is a selfish opportunist with 'big ideas'. Do you agree?
4. Realistically, Ron is the one character who sets an example of how to achieve success. Is this true?
5. 'We cannot let too much concern for others influence the decisions we make for our own well-being'. Which characters would agree with this statement and why?
6. In *Diving for Pearls* Thomson suggests that people need to 'stick together' in order to survive injustice. Do you agree?
7. The only real victim in the play is Verge — she is the one who loses the most. Discuss.
8. The ending of *Diving for Pearls* is appropriately bleak for a play about loss and losers. Discuss.
9. The different ways the other characters relate to Verge give vital information about their personalities and motivations. Do you agree?
10. This play is rich in symbolism. Identify a range of the symbols used and discuss their relevance and importance.

Analysing an Exam Answer

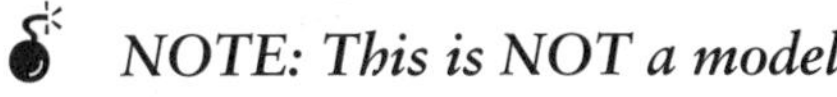

Read the sample answer then discuss the questions below.

Topic 10: The play is rich in symbolism. Identify a range of the symbols used and discuss their relevance and importance.

Answer

Thomson uses not only objects but places and people symbolically in order to help convey her message. When we first meet Den and Barbara they are standing on a hill which overlooks the city where they live. The fact that they are 'looking in' from 'outside' the city helps alert us to their status as exiles — they do not totally belong in some way to the place and its society. Significantly, the play starts and finishes on this hill which tends to reinforce the fact that even though they attempted to belong, Den and Barbara have both wound up as outsiders once again.

The State Engineering Works and the Resort Beach International Resort hotel are also symbolic in that they represent the changing face of the social and economic priorities of the city — and society in general. The steelworks from which Den is eventually excluded stands for an industry that makes a practical contribution to the area. Not only did the Works provide employment for the personnel who manufactured the trains, but it also enabled the on-going employment of the many workers whose labour produced the steel to make the trains and the coal that they carried.

In contrast to 'The Works', the hotel's 'usefulness' to the city appears to be much narrower. We can see from Barbara's heartbreaking experience that the benefits from being a member of its work force will only be enjoyed by a select few. In the same way it becomes obvious that the 'product' which the hotel supplies will, again, only cater to a select, even privileged, domestic market with the majority of its patrons coming from overseas. 'Japs — won't be able to stop themselves. Yanks'll be flying here direct' (Barbara, p. 22) and this helps us to recognise the implications of the differences between a national industry, the State Engineering Works, and a private enterprise, the Resort Beach International Resort.

The house in which Den lives is another symbol. This house stands for the typical Australian home that everyone, regardless of class or financial success, accepts as being achievable. By contrasting it with the workers' cottages that have, virtually 'overnight', become real estate 'goldmines', we realise that when the opportunity for profit presents itself, people are inclined to harden their hearts against the more emotional needs of human beings. For Den, his house represents the tradition of family — it is not a home unless it contains a family to nurture. Barbara, on the other hand, sees a house as a status symbol and as security and to Verge, the dwelling becomes a place in which to enjoy the security of being loved and wanted. Although Marj realises that her house lacks a family to live in it, she nevertheless views it as a symbol that she is a worthwhile member of her society, while Ron and Jeannie see houses in terms of real estate — commodities that represent money, profit and success.

Den's father's tuba is a recurring symbol in the play. It is the 'voice' of Den's father which represents the history of Australia's working class and which raises memories of the hard struggle workers experienced in order to achieve fair conditions and realistic wages. The tuba is an instrument which does not 'stand alone' but performs at its best within an orchestra — as a member of a larger group. This reinforces Thomson's idea that if we cut ourselves off from others we risk the fate of being a 'lone voice' and consequently not being heard, which is Den's fate when he tries to speak to his colleagues at 'the works'. Barbara's remark about the Miners' Federation Band, 'That lot's so old, every time they go out marching someone else drops dead. They've hardly got any instruments left, it's all done with tape-recorders' (p. 24) makes us realise that the younger generation, in no longer seeing themselves as an active, cohesive group, have left themselves vulnerable to destruction by external forces. The band is now supplemented by an artificial voice that reminds us of the taped 'muzak' version of 'The Fool on the Hill' that plays in the unfinished hotel and which emphasises its cold and impersonal characteristics.

Finally, because Thomson's characters are representative without being stereotypical, we are made aware of some of the differences in human attitudes and behaviour that cause a society to become divided into separate classes. Marj stands for those people who, because they do things for others in the name of charity fail to consider that they might be doing more harm than good. Ron depicts the type of person who has succumbed to the 'greed is good' ethic and Barbara reminds us of the large proportion of people who would dearly love to belong to the 'materialistic' society and who will continually be closed out of it. Den characterises the honest, down-to-earth and caring people for whom money and material gain can never replace love and human decency, and Verge portrays the innocent and vulnerable human beings who, sadly, often become the victims of the very society whose responsibility it is to keep them safe.

Discussion Questions

- Does the opening here appropriately focus on the given topic?
- Is a full understanding of the topic readily apparent?
- Does the essay develop logically and sequentially?
- Is appropriate detail from the text provided?
- Is there a sense of personal engagement that involves the reader?

REFERENCES & READING

The Text

Thomson, Katherine, *Diving for Pearls*, Currency Press, Paddington, NSW, 1992.

Reviews

Allen, David, "Doomed love has universal appeal", in *The Australian*, 5 June 1998, p. 15.

Baker, Candida, "'Pearls' from Geelong", in *The Age*, 26 March 1991, p. 14.

Carroll, Steven, Review in *The Age Entertainment Guide*, 22 March 1991, p. 13.

Craven, Peter, "Cardboard cut-outs cast adrift in the shallows", in *The Australian*, 4 April 1991, p. 9.

Croggon, Alison, "Wisdom of Pearls", in *The Bulletin*, v. 113, n. 5765, 16 April 1991, p. 118.

Kiernander, Adrian, "Diving for Pearls", in *The Australian*, 15 October 1993, p. 10.

Litson, Jo, "A writer who plays on poetry", in *The Australian*, 1 April 1991, p. 7.

Mitchell, Marea, "Diving for Pearls", in *The Australian*, 22 July 1994, p. 12.

Neill, Rosemary, "Emotional force lost in slick laughs", *The Australian*, 23 October 1992, p. 9.

Payne, Pamela, "Shoot me, I'm only the writer", interview with Katherine Thomson in *The Bulletin*, v. 113, n. 5762, 26 March 1991, pp. 110-111.

Perkins, Elizabeth, "*The Girl Who Saw Everything* by Alma De Groen and *Diving for Pearls* by Katherine Thomson", in *Australasian Drama Studies*, n. 24, April 1994, pp. 197-200.

Waites, James, "Travails at the Steelworks", in *The Sydney Morning Herald*, 28 August 1995, p. 15.

Ward, Peter, "Diving for Pearls", in *The Australian*, 23 October 1992, p. 9.